SUPERFLOW

SUPERFLOW

LIGHT UP THE ARTIST IN YOU

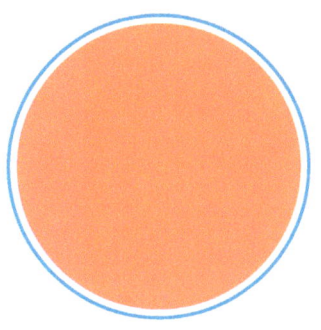

SUSAN CURRIE

SHANTI ARTS PUBLISHING
BRUNSWICK, MAINE

SUPERFLOW
LIGHT UP THE ARTIST IN YOU

Copyright © 2021 Susan Currie
All Rights Reserved
No part of this book may be reproduced in
any manner whatsoever without permission
from the publisher in writing, except for the
inclusion of brief quotations in a review.

Published by Nine Rivers,
–guiding you on your journey–
an imprint of Shanti Arts Publishing

Interior design by Shanti Arts Designs
Cover design by Kara E. Schutte

Shanti Arts LLC
193 Hillside Road
Brunswick, Maine 04011

shantiarts.com

Printed in the United States of America

ISBN: 978-1-951961-95-4 (softcover)

Library of Congress Control Number: 2021940649

"The object of being alive is to contribute to other people. What better way to do that than through an art form?"

— Seymour Bernstein

CONTENTS

INTRODUCTION 11

SANG

ONE
SONG OF YOURSELF **18**
Practice One — Take the One Seat 24

TWO
SUBTRACTION **28**
Practice Two — Catch the Day 34

THREE
GROUNDWORK . . . BRANCHING IN ... **36**
Practice Three — Branching In 42

FOUR
COMPOSING . . . POISE OF MIND **44**
Practice Four — Make It Uncommon 50

FIVE
BREATH TAKING **52**
Practice Five — Breath Taking 56

INTERMISSION 59

GYEY ....

SIX
THOREAUING **64**
Practice Six — Thoreauing 70

SEVEN
WORK, IN PROGRESS **72**
Practice Seven — Outtaking 78

EIGHT
WHO CARES? **82**
Practice Eight — Artist Statement 86

NINE
SHARE THE MERIT **88**
Practice Nine — Be a Lamp 92

TEN
ENCORE! **94**
Practice Ten — Report Card 98

CONCLUSION 103

NOTES 106

ACKNOWLEDGMENTS 109

REPURPOSES 111

ABOUT THE AUTHOR 113

INTRODUCTION

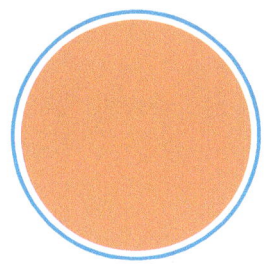

GOOD NEWS... THERE IS NOTHING IN THE NEXT ten chapters you need to memorize! Not ONE thing. So take yourself right off that hook.

This is a book whose teachings are meant to be explored with effort and *also* with a genuine sense of ease. May its pages meet you where you are, wherever you are—emotionally, physically, spiritually, financially, or artistically.

Bring to mind the ocean and, some distance from where you stand on the shore, a swimmer carving the water. Each purposeful stroke appears effortless, dreamlike as they make their way through the current's push and pull. What zone this person is in is impossible to know. Clearly though, beyond a physical strength, there is some higher state of mind in the mix. The swimmer is both reaching for *and* playing to the height of their intelligence. Any and all interference appears to have been silenced.

When a person accesses that state of flow, there is no yawning. Their attention is completely swept up in the present moment, and they operate at their fullest capacity. We can be that swimmer in our art making—in balance, of strong mind and body, clear seeing, and allowing an inner sureness to carry us. We too can enjoy that liquidity of process and break out beyond the ordinary in our creativity.

SUPERFLOW ... *Light Up the Artist in You* is a modern-day playbook for doing so. Creative souls of all levels are welcome on its path.

For decades, my life as a photographer was weighted with plotting. Throughout much of this professional chapter, my creative muscles were clenched—my mind preoccupied by procedure and peers and gear. While this journey was unfolding, I was also working as a yoga instructor. Blindly, I did not see how one completely distant vocation could possibly inform the other.

In my yoga practice, all was much more fluid. Few kept score. On the mat, you take the attention inward, practice a series of postures and sequences, breathe a lot, then repeat all that over and over again for days and weeks and months and such. In doing so, gradually you begin to embody the movements and start to flow through the sequences with a grace and an elevated self-awareness in an autopilot-like mode. The volume on your overthinking dims, and in that absence of chatter you begin to naturally become both posture and sequence. Flow state. There's just a sureness and an uncalculated GO. Game changer in terms of the quality of the experience! Many who practice yoga will attest to this heightened perception and quality of productivity and the seamless manner in which it tends to seep from the mat and into other of life's aspects. Through such osmosis the practice often emerges as a "lifestyle."

One day on my yoga mat I experienced one of those epiphany-like moments I did not see coming. What if I allowed some of these same principles of the ancient eight-limbed practice of yoga to inch into my creative process? The Tibetan term for enlightenment is translated as the union of two words: *sang*, meaning clearing away the delusions and bad habits of the mind; and *gyey*, the developing and bringing forth of our true nature. I don't recall any of my art teachers extending much focus on taking one's attention inward and preparing the mind before getting behind the lens of a camera? But suddenly, it all made perfect sense.

As I further explored this possibility, I began to more fully show up to my creative work. And over time, I found new truths in the art I was making— an uncontrived integrity I had not before met. Art became for me . . . a lifestyle.

That long ago epiphany continues to remind me that flow is not something one can command. There is no "on demand"-type switch. But one can, with effort, create for themselves those conditions that set you up for its arrival. This notion of clearing away and (then) bringing forth ground the **SUPERFLOW** structure. As both a student, teacher, and artist, I have witnessed, among creative souls of all levels and mediums, the transformative power of this duet.

Ehipassiko is a term in the Sanskrit language often translated as, "come see for yourself." I invite you to do so in the pages that follow. **SUPERFLOW**'s ten cumulative chapters are micro in nature—intentionally. My hope is that, in whatever amount of your precious available time, you will pause with each principle, make the concept your very own, play with the uncomplicated exercises offered in each chapter, create the art that only YOU can make, put it out there in service to the world, and then turn back to Chapter One and repeat the sequence again and again. ***I believe in the promise of an art-drenched world. Each and every one of us was born with a hidden super power—the gift of creativity. Let's go flex that might!***

Hope your road is a long one . . .
Keep Ithaka always in your mind.
Arriving there is what you're destined for.
But do not hurry the journey at all.
Better if it lasts for years,
so you're old by the time you reach the island,
wealthy with all you've gained on the way.

—from the poem "Ithaka,"
by Constantine P. Cavafy

SANG

ONE

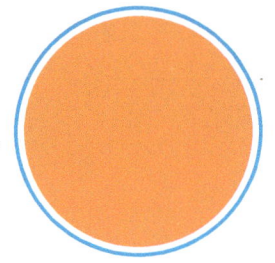

SONG OF YOURSELF

"I just have to keep reminding myself that I am only going to be me, and I'm only ever going to be me. It's such a waste of time to invest in anything else."

—Ben Platt

WE ARE GROOMED FOR GO. BARELY HAS THE light turned from yellow, and off we barrel to next up. **SUPERFLOW**'s aim is to curb that full steam so the work we make—in this case art—might stem from some truer place.

This sequence does not begin with a supply list. In fact, it doesn't call for special materials of any kind. Think of these first chapters—or pillars—not as a slam of the brakes—as in, *now I'm an artist*. Instead, imagine them as a prelude—the prep work before launching into your creative project. Let these pages serve as a tool for pausing and directing your attention inward. In this space of the next few chapters, you just might meet some of the habits and hindrances that are really not serving you and come to understand the source of your perpetual forward lunging. So, hold onto that thought. Bookmark that bright idea for the bestseller. Let's get slow . . .

Well into my creative career, with many unhelpful habits lodged firmly in place, I was introduced to the concept of dharma art through the book *True Perception* by Chögyam Trungpa. I was at once swept up by its common sense. Dharma art essentially translates into "art without aggression." It's not referring to aggression as a physical offense but rather the silent plotting and striving that so often hijack a creative endeavor. **SUPERFLOW** is about creating favorable circumstances in which we might unhijack our piano playing or painting or pirouetting, and flow more freely. Essential to creating this climate is knowing yourself in a clear way and connecting with a definition of YOU that is true today.

"Can't anybody see what I see?" Vincent van Gogh, throughout his career, tormented himself with this inquiry. The answer is, was, and always will be ***NO***. Not precisely. Regardless of gender, race, physical ability, and such, each of us arrives here with our own unique lens and note to play. Can you imagine for a moment if van Gogh, in his brief thirty-seven years, had caved to the conventional, had portrayed someone other than himself, had not honored his true vision or played his note?

Among the many things that curb your accessing this gift of creativity is an inaccurate sense of self. In an effort to reunite with the true you, begin with the question, "Who do I think I am?" Note the emphasis on the first "I" in the probe. Often (for safety reasons), we move about armed with our contrived elevator speeches that spell out some fixed identity. In many cases, these labels or stories have gone unedited for decades. When you were eight, you probably didn't have to give yourself this much thought. Around meals and snacks and siblings, you went to school, played a bit, did some homework, then got into bed. Life was simple. You were a kid, and likely, that's who you thought you were. Then came aging and life and with that came preferences, pitfalls, endless thinking, and rethinking. In that history, imprints and impressions built up and deepened the identity you wrote for yourself and have clung to so preciously.

SUPERFLOW is about creating favorable circumstances in which we might unhijack our piano playing or painting or pirouetting, and flow more freely. Essential to creating this climate is knowing yourself in a clear way, connecting with a definition of YOU that is true today.

Jon Kabat-Zinn, the founder and director of the Stress Reduction Clinic at the University of Massachusetts, reminds us that, **"However old you are, THIS is the perfect moment to find out who you are in the deepest ways."** And he suggests the "who" is not derived from the narratives in our head. Take this chapter to sit with your current definition of self and notice its staying power. There is no wrong or right answer here.

Bring to mind a few people in your life and recall the abbreviated identities by which you have come to know them ***and*** how those long running labels confine and mute the multitudes of their character. *Sarah is the oldest of five. Sophia is an introvert. George is the technical one. Lindsay is an only child. Randy is the black sheep of the family. Kelly has both a law degree and an MBA.* This probe is meant, simply, as an accuracy exercise, a pause in which you might fact check this internal classification of you. While it may have resembled you at one point, how accurate is this identity right now?

> Who might you be if you eased, edited, or unloaded altogether the self-imposed facade? The reply is for your eyes only. WANDER IN, WHOLLY AND KINDLY. See how your definition surfaces and its contour shifts over the gift of some single-pointed concentration.

Not only does the role playing exhaust us, but these masks and fictions about who we are fuel the very type of aggression about which Trungpa cautions. When left unchecked they source the choke of our true nature. Essence is a seven-letter word for something only you can see.

Why is it smart to befriend your truest you? So as you progress creatively, you hear and express only that—vividly. Who might you be if you eased, edited, or unloaded altogether the self-imposed facade? The reply is for your eyes only. Wander in, wholly and kindly. See how your definition surfaces and its contour shifts over the gift of some single-pointed concentration. Over the next nine **SUPERFLOW** pillars, commit to tending to this new version of you, so you might then go BE that person!

From this hour I ordain myself loos'd of limits and imaginary lines,
Going where I list, my own master total and absolute,
Listening to others, considering well what they say,
Pausing, searching, receiving, contemplating,
Gently, but with undeniable will, divesting myself of the holds that would hold me
I inhale great draughts of space,
The east and the west are mine, and the north and the south are mine.

— Walt Whitman

Practice One — **Take the One Seat**

Pick a room, any room in your home or office or space of choice. In an intentional manner, place two chairs beside one another. Take a seat in one. Allow your eyes to close as you land in your seated position.

Enjoy a few moments of inhaling and exhaling, allowing the breath to anchor you and reign in any scattered energies.

You might call upon your relaxed breath and kindly scan your body, beginning with the crown of the head and the muscles in the face, easing the shoulders, and then with each breath traveling that attention right down into the soles of your feet.

Begin to bring this question—
Who do I think I am?
—into your consciousness. Let the answer unfold naturally without trying to fix anything. Does this image suit you today? Notice how this identity feels internally. Are there tensions arising in areas of the body where there may have been ease? Just notice what you notice and continue to enjoy your quiet.

In your own time, deepen the breath and allow some small movement back into the body, circling out the shoulders or the neck, and then blinking open your closed eyes. As you come back into the place you are seated, take a moment to stand, and with a sense of sureness, leave that seat behind and take your place in the other chair. Envision this act as severing ties with the person who had been seated there.

As you assume this new perch, again return to the breath. Let it be carefree and uncontrolled.

Begin to listen for and visualize a new you.

The weight of that "other" now lifted, notice who surfaces. Breathe in that clean slate of you with each inhale. At the finish of each exhale, rest in the gap. In that space

welcome the new empty vessel that is you.

Stay there as long as you like. When you are ready, deepen the breath and again allow some small movement back into the body.

As you come back into the place you are seated, take a moment to

**stand
with
your
new
possibility.**

> *To look closely with the attention of questioning changes everything.*
> *—Jane Hirshfield*

TWO

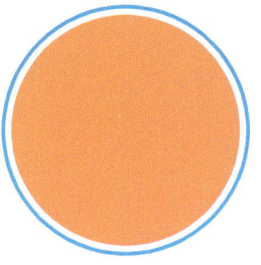

SUBTRACTION

> *"Everything that makes more of you than you have ever been, even in your best hours, is right."*
> —Rainer Maria Rilke

THE PURPOSE OF WEALTH MANAGEMENT IS TO coordinate assets so they work in harmony, thus achieving higher yields. These principles are not restricted to coins and cash. Weeks and days and hours and moments are a wealth that warrants an equal course chart.

When you apply a similar logic to the currency that is your daily twenty-four hours, you safeguard that brand-new self to which you are acclimating. Harmony and higher yields and peace are all possible, and a path to them begins with subtraction—a far too underutilized tool. It's the opposite of addition. As you continue to clear away, prepare the mind, and meet the promise of your true verses, it's time to employ some simple math. Jack Kerouac championed the **"big blank potential,"** which we each own. Is that being met by you? Let's get intentional about the nonessentials that swipe up a day—those things that are simply not adding value to your well-being.

For many of us, there's an ongoing interior theft

happening everyday. Nobody cares for the feeling of being cheated. It clenches the mind, body, and especially the spirit. In a fog, we watch from the sidelines as the best of us gets snatched up Sunday through Sunday. We blame it on technology or the universal quest to be productive or countless other hooks. We could instead take responsibility and remember we have a say in the matter.

Have you looked up at the sky today? Subtraction is the mighty trick for reclaiming small portions of our (choked) fixed twenty-four hours. It begins with saying "no more" and "no, thank you" to those responsibilities, commitments, myths, invitations, bad habits, and assorted other detractors that make less of you, instead of more. You are hereby granted the authority to get careful and intentional about your precious time and to edit one or more of these bandits from your day. **"How we spend our days is, of course, how we spend our lives. A schedule defends from chaos and whim. It is a net for catching days,"** observed Annie Dillard in the pages of her book *The Writing Life*. Subtraction in this instance is not so much a call to plot out a daily schedule to fill but instead a suggestion (or nudge) to study the value of all that we heap onto our days—and to do something about it.

On a thought, I recently reached out to a highly accomplished printmaker and textile artist whose work I greatly admire. I was hoping this individual might have some interest in collaborating on a project I had in mind. Without offering any specific details on my idea, I simply said "hello"

SUBTRACTION is the mighty trick for reclaiming small portions of our (choked) fixed twenty-four hours. It begins with saying "no more" and "no, thank you" to those responsibilities, commitments, myths, invitations, bad habits, and assorted other detractors that make less of you, instead of more.

electronically and floated the prospect of our working in concert creatively. With a prompt and graceful reply, she declined. "While I'm incredibly flattered, I have chosen to focus my work on specific types of projects." I was, of course, disappointed in the gentle "nay," but I so respected her "no, thank you." Her sense of purpose was as an excellent illustration of subtraction, of someone protecting their commitment to their personal creative path and confidently averting any disturbance to their brushstroke. There was no pondering the invite on her part or following up in search of more information on its arrangement; it was a firm decision to fend off interruption.

In 1858, in order to study the cattle sent for consumption in France, the French engineer Charles Joseph Minard became one of the first to use a pie chart. Remember the pie chart? Those bright slices of color designed to communicate relative sizes of data? In addition to tracking cattle consumption, their analog nature serves as a handy tool for recognizing the reality of our days. It all begins with a circle (or pie) drawn on a blank sheet of the paper of your choice

First step is to back out all of the non-negotiable events of the day: sleeping, eating, work, childcare, dog walking, etc. Carve a truthful slice out for each of these activities. From the remains, portion out other mostly essential elements: laundry, connecting with friends, grooming, housekeeping, etc. In doing so, put YOU first. Remember the idea is to reclaim some authority over how you spend your days. Now sit with your chart and notice where you see space. In these open slices lies your freedom and your power. These spaces offer a refuge in your day—a golden opportunity to thoughtfully and carefully add those

> Remember the idea is to RECLAIM SOME AUTHORITY OVER HOW YOU SPEND YOUR DAYS . . . These spaces offer a refuge in your day—a golden opportunity to thoughtfully and carefully add those things that make more of you than you have ever been. These reclaimed moments for breathing are precious.

things that make more of you than you have ever been. These reclaimed moments for breathing are precious. Keep them as so. Make THESE spaces your new non-negotiables.

not merely . . .

i am keeping time in courts
centers, where things flourish
where things live fully, not merely
what shall i ignore today,
in order to build true verses?

what noise can i mute
to be still, to be silent
among the shaded detail, the subtle gradations
and let the morning, the garden, the lone white birch
come to me

all in due time
is this not how we paint nocturnes?

Two — Catch the Day

Set aside some uncluttered time and space for getting present and connecting with your breath. Grab a sketchbook or notebook with some blank pages and sit on a back porch or elsewhere—out-of-doors if possible. Take some cues from the earth and the elements as you take your attention inward. What might the breeze be suggesting, or the late afternoon sunshine? Is there birdsong or some other soundtrack being supplied by the natural world? What does the soundscape bring up for you?

Allow your mind and spirit the gift of an unhurried segue in. As cued on the previous pages, make your circle and begin to carve its slices. Notice what you notice, such as any tightening that happens in the body or mind as you move into the (mostly) "essential-moment" slices. If you do notice

tension or tightening, go deeper and
weigh the urgency of this slice.

Could it be subtracted?

A smile or ease of breath as you allot
your slices is a good indicator of a
portion's added value. As you finish
up, make note of the open space.
Even a sliver should be looked at as
progress in your day-catching.

**Take a few breaths to celebrate
the fact that you were able
to snatch back time for
some of the best of you.**

Remember, this chart is not a schedule.
It is meant to serve as a fact-check
practice. Make a kind commitment
to make this newfound slice of soul
time just as essential as your sleeping
and eating and dog-walking.

THREE

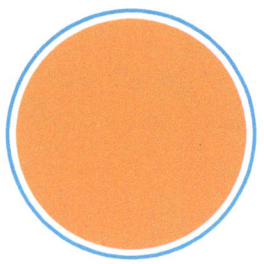

GROUNDWORK... BRANCHING IN

"In solitude...we love the flowers, the grass and the waters and the sky. In the motion of the very leaves of spring in the blue air there is then found a secret correspondence with our heart."

—Percy Shelley

ONE OF THE RICHEST LESSONS I KNOW IS TO STAND under a thriving tree—in any season, in any weather—and be drenched in its glorious multitudes. The limbs and blooms of an oak or a pine or a banyan steal the show, but it's their long chapter of grounding and inner work that makes the brilliance possible. Decades of grit and poise and strength training fuel that single cardinal leaf that flutters from the branch and quivers the heart on a late autumn morning.

There is much to borrow from a tree's discipline and slow manner of living. While our culture preaches networking and branching out, trees demonstrate that in order to be skillful and alive in such extension, some level of staying put and branching inward is a prerequisite. **"We're always fascinated with something in the beginning, and we would like to cultivate that fascination and brew it and drink it until**

we get intoxicated," points out Chögyam Trungpa in the pages of his book *True Perception.* **"In order for art to be certain and definite and workable, I would say that you definitely need sitting practice as basic pre-art training. It's the only way you don't distort,"** he concludes. Getting quiet, in whatever shape this repose takes for you, is integral to the success of the **SUPERFLOW** approach. In the sustained nourishment of our inward self, an essential sureness begins to sprout.

Kathleen Clemons is an award-winning photographer, teacher, and author. She is widely revered for her gift of sculpting light into sublime images of flowers and the natural world. A confidence of vision enables her to get completely consumed, losing herself in line and color and shape while out scouting her subjects along the coast of her native Maine. Speaking of her approach to shooting, she puts it this way, **"It's just me and a flower and bliss."** That lack of interference between her and her subject is precisely the X factor that makes magical her dahlias and daisies. Such certitude is something we each can access when we develop it and connect with it by branching in.

Where I would swerve slightly from Trungpa's wise coaching is with the "sitting" aspect. Meditation or contemplative practice of some fashion does not necessarily need to look like sitting still. Groundwork is not a one-size-fits-all part of the **SUPERFLOW** training. The majority of my brightest ideas arrive unannounced in motion out on my morning walks. ***Silence + Breathing + Repetition*** is my personal equation. I began these walks years ago with physical fitness as the goal, and over time the miles began to take on a rather sacred quality. In that ritual state, I began to connect with myself and find my wonder. When I began to explore a spiritual path over two decades ago, I never would have imagined that my inward branching would look like moving out among life's bustle for extended periods of time. But that is where I find my personal quiet, where I begin to make my pictures and my poems.

Please go see for yourself what works. The philosopher Alex Soojung Kim Pang, in his book *Rest*, writes, **"A routine creates a landing place for the muse."** The idea is to lay the foundation for some ritual that for you unlatches a gate inward, and in that clearing you tend to your interior. How do YOU sort yourself out? Where is that place or space or practice in which you can breathe most freely? What is the activity or inactivity that brings back balance? When was the last time you blazed your own trail in response to such questions? In the previous practice (Catch the Day),

> Look to the tree whose roots are flourishing and foundation solid, and you will notice brilliance and blooming and majesty regardless of the weather. When the interior is tended to, not only are we boosting the development of a SOLID FOUNDATION or trunk but also nourishing our internal system of roots that consists of VISION and WONDER and SELF-CONFIDENCE and DISCERNMENT, among other things.

you claimed back a small space of your day for your personal well-being. Fill it up playing with this probe.

In the ancient eight-limbed practice of yoga, one of the essential "landing" poses to which one returns again and again on the mat is *tadasana* or mountain pose. *Tadasana* is a standing pose of dignity where one is instructed to breath deeply; connect with the ground; lift the heart; roll the shoulders up, back, and down; and imagine a slight lift to the crown area of the head—elongated and strong like a mountain. Instant royalty! Conscious breathing coupled with some subtle shifts to our habitual upright posture have a way of magically elevating the vertical experience.

Silence + Breathing + Repetition
Silence + Breathing + Repetition
Silence + Breathing + Repetition
Silence + Breathing + Repetition
Silence + Breathing + Repetition
Silence + Breathing + Repetition

Could something as effortless as this serve as your ongoing inward branching practice? Another such exercise ever at our disposal is a daily gratitude practice. Make simple your branching in. Again, the idea is to weave it in as a way of life.

Revisit again the tree metaphor to note the distinction between **growing** and **growing well as a creative soul**. Healthy root systems are lifelines for woody perennials. Look to the tree whose roots are flourishing and foundation solid, and you will notice brilliance and blooming and majesty regardless of the weather. When the interior is tended to, not only are we boosting the development of a solid foundation (or trunk) but also nourishing our internal system of roots that is comprised of vision and wonder and self-confidence and discernment, among other things. Such an inner resilience is essential armor in the ongoing confusion that is the artist's life.

While this pillar of the **SUPERFLOW** sequence might appear as a bit of a snooze, the cumulative effects of this seemingly unhistoric effort will provide much sustenance as you produce and share your art. Like the unprotected tree out your window, expect to be assailed regularly on your creative path as it unfolds. Among your stormy weather will be doubt and distortion, critique and competition, blank pages and "we've decided to pass at this time." In these adverse moments, you will be less likely to get hooked and detoured thanks to your slowly churned mettle and the immunity and clarity it delivers. If you are content making ordinary art, skimp on your groundwork. If you want to make extraordinary art, trouble yourself to do the groundwork. It's a noble pursuit that has the power to change everything.

> When the interior is tended to, not only are we boosting the development of a solid foundation (or trunk) but also nourishing our internal system of roots that is comprised of vision and wonder and self-confidence and discernment.

Practice Three — **Branching In**

Make a commitment to practice for four or five successive days—indoors or out. Begin by reconnecting with your breath and exhaling any thoughts or worries that are not of service to your well-being. Let your conscious breathing anchor you. Five deep inhales accompanied by outward sighs might help to shed some of the weight of your mind. On day one, you might borrow the previously mentioned mountain pose exercise for five minutes. Tune into your posture, scan the body, unbend your eyebrows, and notice any other areas where you are feeling a clench. Eyes can be open or closed, depending on your balance and comfort level. Find your *tadasana*, and allow each inhale and exhale to ground you deeper into the pose. Get silent. Take a cue from the poet Frank O'Hara who wrote, "Listen to the air becoming no air, becoming air again."

On days two through four or five, again claim that nonnegotiable well-being slice of your day. Use this time to experiment with other practices for going inward and toning the mind and spirit. Make them super simple and keep some score. In these practices, ask yourself if you are breathing a little or a lot. Which of these activities propels you close to a TEN in terms of ease of mind? Can you see yourself (reasonably) making one of them a habit? As coached earlier in this **SUPERFLOW** limb, make simple your practice. This exercise is not to be confused with finding a hobby. Closing your eyes and sitting quietly with a piece of music, reading a poem, taking a bicycle ride, walking the poodle, lighting a candle, lacing up your rollerblades and gliding through the breeze, making a cup of tea. What is the activity that brings you back to balance?

FOUR

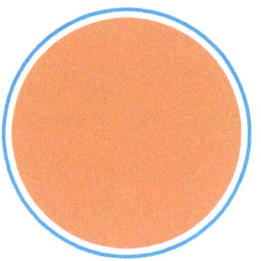

COMPOSING . . . POISE OF MIND

"Listen to the hummingbird whose wings you cannot see. Listen to the hummingbird, don't listen to me. Listen to the butterfly whose days but number three. Listen to the butterfly, don't listen to me."

—Leonard Cohen

EDWARD WESTON, ONE OF THE MASTERS OF twentieth-century photography, suggested that **"Composition is the strongest way of seeing."** This act of combining elements in order to form a more brilliant whole is by no means restricted to a camera's viewfinder. Yet the theater of the mind first needs to be harmonized before such lucidity is possible. The previous **SUPERFLOW** pillar found us committing to a regular contemplative habit. Now let's make a pact to permit the present to take precedent over all other while in this hallowed space. You might frame this principle as a kind of "falling into" arrangement.

> The enormous full moon dropped its milk light through the skylight like a rope ladder that spread across my Chinese rug and the edge of my quilt. Everything

> was still. I read with the aid of a battery-powered lantern that projected a white rainbow across the objects arranged on the bookcase not six feet from my bed. The rain was hammering the skylight. I felt the trepidation of October's end, magnified by the waxing moon and a commemoration of storms assembling in the sea.

On page 148 of her book *M Train*, in a chapter entitled "Her Name Was Sandy," Patti Smith shared this language with her reader. She was laying down her scene of place in the approaching storm, Hurricane Sandy. Her cinematic sentences, so rich in metaphor, plant the reader right beside the author under the skylight and the "hammering" rain. Language like this simply does not happen without poise of mind. So . . . we compose. We make a regular appointment with ourself to combine those elements, discussed and practiced in previous chapters, that we have been forming—Catch the Day and Branching In. In building upon and blending these practices, an inner muscle memory begins to take root. In its toning, a valuable reserve for approaching our creative work begins its pool. As the muscle further matures and our awareness of the spaces and scenes we occupy expands, we too can come to notice and name "white rainbows" and "commemorations of storms."

Perhaps an idea for an art project has recently surfaced or some small seeds of an idea. Maybe there's a question that keeps coming up for you. Start to take that imagination (or inquiry) with you into your regular Branching In practice. No agenda, no outline, no attachment to results. With some intention, just allow these sparks into your consciousness. While you're out on your early evening run or deep in your forest walk and the deluge of commitments and hindrances begins its swell, meet that volume with some dreaming. Permit your wonder to elbow that noise to the background. Notice things. Every observation reveals a metaphor to be uncovered.

After years of city living and slowly earning his stripes in the music world, the indie-rock multi-instrumentalist, singer, and songwriter Andrew Bird, traded in his amplified Chicago life for the repose of a red-trimmed countryside barn set amidst silence and acres of corn and soybeans. He was seeking a **"step away from the density of his urban existence"** to soothe a lingering restlessness and perhaps compose himself in some truer way. There, in his three-year solitary adventure, by listening to his neighboring cows, studying the changing weather systems, communing with cumulus clouds as they drifted in and faded out over the fields, and measuring space, he recalibrated what he was seeing and uncovered new ways to hear the music he was making. As he

> NOTICE THINGS. Every observation reveals a metaphor to be uncovered.

planted himself in this new landscape, time slowed down and he began to notice relationships, such as the way he looked at a tree and how that vision imprinted a spareness to the new music he began to craft. Framing his voice into loops, whistling in silos, and often relying on only two chords or notes, Bird started to musically project out what was happening inside of him—intuitively. "Go to a place where you can hear yourself. And, if you can hear it, then you can make it sing" is the teaching he uncovered in his sojourn. "Hearing yourself" is by no means a breeze. Bird spent three unplugged years alone under aged timber and purple skies in an effort to do so. Finally, though, his dedication proved fruitful; with no awareness of an audience, he arrived at the signature sound for which he is most critically acclaimed.

New York City-based Jenny Kroik is an accomplished illustrator, painter, and art instructor. She credits a decade-long meditation practice with improving her ability to sit at her desk and stay put. "When I paint, I often feel that all my negative thoughts get louder, and sitting at my desk can be almost unbearable at times. Some of the most unbearable thoughts are often about the 'uselessness' of the art practice, and I often feel the need to reply to those thoughts, to try to justify my right to do something essentially 'useless'."

Over time, meditation has enhanced Kroik's ability to extend her painting sessions and concentration, thus allowing her to polish her technique through consistent practice. "Sitting longer allowed me to

> Get comfortable with slow... sculpt yourself some poise of mind, allowing for the common to begin, through your cleared lens, to BECOME UNCOMMON.

add a lot more detail, and work on more complex pictures that would stress me out before." These "more complex" pictures have, in recent years, graced the cover of the *New Yorker* as well as the pages of countless other publications.

Today Jenny equates her process of making art to an extended meditation practice and feels less driven by "success" each time she sits down to paint her stories. **"Meditation helped me to understand what's happening inside my mind, and helped me to observe it objectively, rather than getting exhausted arguing with myself every time I wanted to sit at my desk and do creative work."**

Just keep showing up with your open mind and noticing what you notice. Mary Oliver put it well with this advice: **"Things take the time they take."** The purpose here is to get comfortable with slow. And in the time bend, sculpt yourself some poise of mind, allowing for the common to begin, through your cleared lens, to become uncommon.

Practice Four — **Make It Uncommon**

"In the wholeheartedness of concentration, world and self begin to cohere. With that state comes an enlarging of what may be known, what may be felt, what may be done." Something lovely to chew on from the poet Jane Hirshfield as you begin this exercise.

While such a state of wholeheartedness cannot be flipped on, in practice you can begin to lay some conditions in which such cohesion may come knocking. Set aside fifteen to twenty minutes to unplug from your day's demands. Plunk yourself somewhere with a scene—a still life or a view to which you can latch your attention. You could also, alternatively, pull up some visual on your desktop or enlist a photograph as your field of study. The subject is of little matter for these purposes. The more uncontrived, though, the better. Take note of your start time and perhaps have on hand a free page in a notebook or journal for recording your experience. Allow some mindful breathing to center you as you begin to drop anchor into this exercise. As many times as your mind wanders off, lean on the breath to corral it back. Take a few quiet minutes to arrive fully. Then, if your eyes are closed, flutter them back open and turn your attention to your chosen visual. Over the next twenty or so minutes, make the common uncommon by listing twenty-seven (yes, twenty-seven) truths about the scene before you. Imagine your mind being three-dimensional. Get cinematic. Work in slow motion, resisting the reflex to report the obvious. Breathe easy, and go all in with your senses. There is no limit on time here. As many times as your mind wanders off, return to the breath and fetch it back. Dig deep, work slowly, and chisel out the extraordinary.

FIVE

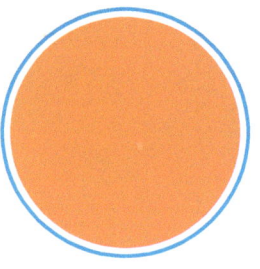

BREATH TAKING

"We have so many allies in this world...including just the color blue in the sky."
—David Whyte

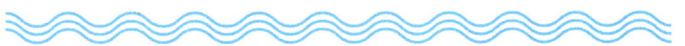

IN EVERY MOMENT COMES THE CHOICE TO FUEL your mind with fuss and drama—or with peace. Allies fall in with the latter. Much higher nutritional value! They burn clean. Allies are the people and the things and the experiences that have your back. Not only do they have your back, allies cooperate and inspire and trade in mutual benefit. Bring to mind something as breathtaking as the freely offered backlit clouds in summer's early evening sky. For your pleasure, there they are. You only need to look up and remember that view as your collaborator.

A mind can be stretched in infinite directions, and you have a big say in the compass points. In which direction shall they be nudged? There are no term limits when it comes to inner growth. Everyday you can be a student living the questions. Getting deliberate around this expansion is integral in both discovering and creating your own sound. **"Read good books, have good sentences in your ears,"** advises the poet Jane Kenyon. This diet extends out into all forms of art. Here's where allies factor into play.

In turning the dial toward your allies, you can begin to reclaim control over the entertainment (or other input) coming at your ears and eyes. First up... technology. What if you were to interrupt your nightly Netflix drama binging with a documentary film? Can you pick one or two days of the week when you pause your playlist in favor of a podcast on your commute into work or your thirty minutes on the treadmill? We live in a land rich with dynamic content, and many of these conversations zero directly in on the artistic process, resulting in an avalanche of ideas and hacks ripe for the snatching. Here's another thought... pause the Twitter or Facebook scrolling, and populate your Instagram feed not with celebrities and influencers. Instead, on social media go find the quiet ones sharing words and images and insights that genuinely light you up.

"Many of our days should be spent, not in vain expectations and lying on our oars, but in carrying out deliberately and faithfully the hundred little purposes which every man's genius must have suggested to him," wrote Henry David Thoreau some two hundred years ago. In other areas of your life, living your **"purposes"** might look like swapping out some of that sofa time for field trips—visiting a local gallery or museum, engaging in an afternoon of live music, taking yourself to a forest or a farm. How about getting an old-fashioned library card and starting to make regular dates in the art or memoir stacks? You could go solo or enlist a field trip buddy on any of these adventures if that will support you in your forays. What are you noticing in these expeditions? What snatches away your breath . . . really seizes it?

Identify artists whose vision or voice pierces your soul, then go follow them. Find out all you can from their work, their path, and their process. At times, stretch from your zone of comfort and know too what you can of opposing voices and art forms—those that do not instinctively call to you. Reflection in the midst of such new voices challenges assumptions and widens the optics through which we see. **"The best things I've learned were NOT content. They were some sort of contrast with someone else's way of thinking that at first seemed really strange to me,"** says author and rabbi Ariel Burger. **"And I, through that process, became aware of my own assumptions and the lens through which I was looking."**

Continuing Education is another adventure you may find useful in finding your frequency or keeping current. From online courses to in-person workshops, to camera and writing clubs, there is rich community to be built and wisdom to be gathered in these settings.

Amidst all of this fueling up and breath taking, be sure to bring a notebook everywhere you go. Record words, colors, quotes, faces, soundscapes, landscapes, billboard copy, song lyrics. **"You were made and set here to give voice to this, your own astonishment,"** says Annie Dillard. Note all the things that strike you when you are out drenching yourself. These notes and jottings and quotes and records you make will serve as power sparks when you begin to make those first brushstrokes or sketch out your opening scenes.

Practice Five — **Breath Taking**

One of the world's most sought after fashion photographers, Paolo Roversi, puts it just so when he says,

"Your artistic style is not something technical . . . at the end, your style is your soul. You don't need to search for it."

The discipline, or challenge, is to connect with it.

After sitting with the suggestions in this chapter, grab a notebook or blank sheet of paper and set aside some time at the end of a day to reconnect with your breath and get quiet. Before beginning, gift yourself a few minutes to sigh away the mind's clutter and get present for this practice. Perhaps playing some quiet music or reading a line of poetry or taking in the evening sky might provide a segue.

As the mind begins to settle, divide the blank page into two columns—one labeled "ally" and the other "foe." Begin to take some stock in the day that you are just finishing. Use your imagination to truthfully populate each column based on the day's events, experiences, and encounters. Notice any reactions or responses in your heart or with your breath as you designate the allies and foes of your day. Pay close attention to those experiences and encounters that resonate as a ballast.

Repeat this activity for a few days in a row, allowing the process to imprint over time. Call on this aptitude as you explore the consumption shifts discussed in this chapter.

INTERMISSION

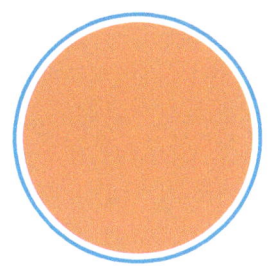

Now is a wonderful time to enjoy some transitional space, to salute the effort made thus far, and to gear up before shifting into the physical act of artistically bringing forth what is beautiful for you. The previous chapters have been spent clearing away, tempering the swell coming at you, and preparing the mind . . . all for the purpose of setting you up in a ready position.

Think of an athlete you admire. I'll take Roger Federer. Be it in practice or on Centre Court at set point, rarely is he seen casually drifting about the baseline in advance of that green sphere of felt soon approaching at 120–160 mph. Rather, he is crouched attentively with his right hand softly gripping the racket and his left at the racket's throat. Next, a quick racket twirl to ease up tension, followed by a split step . . . then showtime. All the while his eyes remain velcroed to the ball. To which side of his racquet that tennis ball will soon land, Roger does not know. Yet in his ready stance, there he waits... supremely prepared for either. That fluidity and single-pointed concentration launches him steps ahead before the ball even enters into play.

By now the merits of being in such a ready position should be coming clear for you. You've done some interior recalibrating. There is a wind at your back. You may have a fairer sense of just who you are. You've claimed back some small portion of your waking hours and dedicated that space to reconnecting with your soul. Your lens is opening wider. You are befriending silence and stillness and beginning to hear the news that arrives in it. You're becoming reacquainted with those things that speak to your soul. These upgrades comprise your headstart as you now step up to creatively return the muse's serve. Whether she arrives at your backhand or forehand, you have set in place the conditions that will support you as you go and make masterpieces.

GYEY

SIX

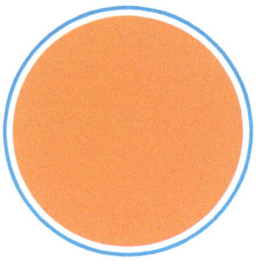

THOREAUING

"The contemplation of things as they are, without error or confusion, without substitution or imposture, is in itself a nobler thing than a whole harvest of invention."

—Francis Bacon

IN MARCH OF 1845 HENRY DAVID THOREAU went to the woods in an effort to live more "deliberately." Back then he said, **"Wherever men have lived there is a story to be told, and it depends chiefly on the storyteller whether that is interesting or not."** To Thoreau, experiencing things forward and back, inside and out, and over and under were as essential as breathing. He was a storyteller supreme, a master of the three-dimensional life and of staying astonished.

Thoreau also shared this: **"I can express adequately only the thought which I love to express—all the faculties in repose but the one you are using—the whole energy concentrated in that."** By this point you should be traveling in the lane of your object of beauty—that subject, theme, or place that fully consumes your imagination. The time has come to tether yourself to it . . . to take a page from Thoreau. Go there, get quiet, stay put, get curious, go back again tomorrow and the next day. Stalk it. Essence is *also* a seven-letter word for something only you can hear. Why not hear it at its most vivid?

The fine art photographer and best-selling author Joyce Tenneson notes that a deep (advance) dive into her subjects is an essential investment in the finished project. Hers takes the shape of endless hours, well in advance of stepping behind the lens, spent communing with the exotic fabrics and backdrops and gifts of the natural world that figure so prominently in her ethereal images. Tenneson finds that creating a dedicated space of standing in quiet conversation with her styling materials enables her to best tease out her vision and surrender to its revelation. Thus she creates portraits that are "something more than the sum of its parts." Her goal always is to go for the TEN. "I truly believe that a TEN out of TEN is not something you can will into existence. There has to be some magic that happens in the process. Whether you are photographing a flower or a person or a tree or a landscape, it can't be simply what everyone else sees. There has to be something unique about it that comes from your own inner self." Certain she has done all the work she can to prepare in advance, Tenneson's extended pre-shoot practice then pushes her into a new realm at show time, one during which she is totally free to communicate the beauty she sees.

> Go there, get quiet, stay put, get curious, go back again tomorrow and the next day. Stalk it. Essence is *also* a seven-letter word for something only you can hear. Why not hear it at its most vivid?

Some element of mystery exists in every person, place, or thing that crosses your path. Remembering this truth refreshes the mind and enables you to bestow upon these encounters a royal quality. Suzuki Roshi, the Japanese Zen master, referred to this state of not knowing as **Beginner's Mind**—a mind not yet made up, one that welcomes the questions. In modeling such a mind and admitting you "don't know," you begin to usher in a higher definition to that person, place, or thing unfolding before you. A probe I love to present to my subjects is, "Tell me one thing you do NOT know." I can generally count on it to stump the person on its receiving end. You may find getting deeper with this query of some use as you practice getting vivid. As you stalk your subject(s), can you confess to ten things about them that you do not know. Then, go forage for your answers?

Staying astonished can be a wonderful exercise in play. If your medium is photography and your stalking is typically carried out behind the lens, leave the camera at home on some days. Instead, bring a sketch pad and some colored pencils and stay tethered through this route. If you are a writer, unpack the journal or keyboard, and swap those out for a watercolor tablet and some paints. Alter the hour of your "stalking" by visiting with your thing of wonder in the evening, instead of at the day's breaking.

There's a term for a segment of the visitors who make their once in a lifetime pilgrimage to the mighty Grand Canyon. After investing the time and effort it takes to arrive there, these folks stand at the rim and have a look, maybe post a few images, and then determine they have seen enough. The locals call them "rimmers." In your creative pursuits, there is no room for rimming. You can NEVER see enough of the subject or concept you mean to express. The extraordinary is not built on swift glimpses. It is

> The extraordinary is not built on swift glimpses. It is born of staying. In order to know a thing and make it come alive in some signature manner, you need to plumb its depths. Let that saturation take the time it takes.

born of staying. In order to know a thing and make it come alive in some signature manner, you need to plumb its depths. Let that saturation take the time it takes. I once heard prayer described as an attention of the heart. That may be a useful metaphor as you wonder what about this thing astonishes you? There is no shortcut here. Wholly calibrate yourself to your subject. The return on that investment will pleasantly surprise you time and time again. The poet Mary Oliver charged that, **"Attention without feeling is only a report."** No one wants to read a report.

> **Creative work needs solitude. It needs concentration without interruptions. It needs the whole sky to fly in, and no eye watching until it comes to that certainty which it aspires to, but does not necessarily have at once.**
>
> —Mary Oliver

Practice Six — **Thoreauing**

THOREAUING is a verb I patched together some time ago. I # it in my social media posts while practicing my "stalking." It keeps my barreling forward in check and reminds me to lock in and stay put.

This exercise salutes Thoreau's mastery. To lean on his wisdom once more:

"Be ever so little distracted—your thoughts so little confused—Your engagements so few—your attention so free your existence so mundane—that in all places and in all hours you can hear the sound of crickets in those seasons when they are to be heard."

Go be with one of your favorite things— subjects or people. Make a commitment of some reasonable amount of time, and attend to only that. Be a mind not yet made up. Set a timer if that helps you to stay put. Get quiet and breathe. What is this thing not telling you? Question it, and from it, tease out some new story—fact or fiction.

How can you stretch it? How can it stretch you?

You might get out of your comfort medium for this exercise. If your preferred medium is writing, tell your story with the camera on your mobile device. If you're a painter, pick up a pen or keyboard and play with writing. If you are a musician, pull out some pastels and tell its story visually.

SEVEN

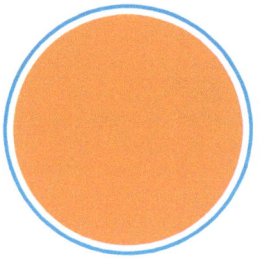

WORK, IN PROGRESS

"Making my art is very serious play. I do have fun, I suppose, but it's more of a sense of discovery than fun. The closest experience I can link it to is when I am in the library looking for something and it leads me to something else. I go from one book to another, and suddenly six hours have passed and I've been off in another world that I knew nothing about…I have a sense of discovery that's extraordinary."
—Donald Lipski

Practice is work … in service of progress. It is the day-to-day, slow tending to your craft by following your questions with a willingness to be surprised as they lead you to places. The last several pillars have brought you to a ready position. Your someday is now here. The ground has been prepared, and it's time now to pick up the brush, sit down at your loom, open the camera's shutter wide, practice, and begin to pour your light. Bring all of the records you've made along your way as you push off and go travel as far as your imagination takes you.

Turning once more to the wisdom of photographer Paolo Roversi, he likens his joy of

> The ground has been prepared, and it's time now to pick up the brush, sit down at your loom, open the camera's shutter wide, practice and begin to pour your light. Bring all of the records you've made along your way as you push off and go travel as far as your IMAGINATION takes you.

making pictures to an endless childhood and that luxury of immersing oneself in an activity about which you are completely passionate. Back when I was eight or so, I would spend hours drawing at the small desk in my bedroom with my records playing. Mostly, I would attempt, over and over, to recreate the album cover of the particular 33 in rotation on my blue (extremely analog) plastic Panasonic turntable. When I tired of my drawing, I would read the album's liner notes and lyrics front to back and back again. The margins to my day were wide, and I was mostly free to stay astonished in my music. Becharmed and content, none of it felt to me like effort. There was no outline or endgame. I was decades removed from recognizing this amusement as a thing called practice. Looking back on the script that has been my life and linking back to those early interests, I see clearly the seeds of my wonder for language and lyric and imagery. Because of who I am, playing with words and pictures is the portal for living and sharing what is best in me.

No one can tell you what to make or how to make your art. With this you are on your own; I like to think that's for the better. Your rhymes and your paintings and your shapes will spring from all the places within you that you have gotten to know over the last six chapters. Many paths diverge in any given experience. Resting for just a moment in that space and **then** placing your hands back on the steering wheel will make for you all of the difference.

East is the direction toward which the Earth rotates its axis and, therefore, the general direction from which the sun appears to rise. In many spiritual traditions, east (or 90 degrees) is the direction to which one ideally orients oneself. You might think of it as home, a place with which you are familiar, or an energy field where you are liquid. It is not 45 degrees, or 125 degrees. You will know east when you land there. It feels like flow. True east is 90, the whole you, the best you, that space in which you get majestic. It's the direction to which you want to be inclined as you work in progress and practice your art. You may find EAST to be a helpful benchmark in your creative practice.

Roversi is revered for his mastery at putting all of himself into the portraits he makes. He explains, "The most important moment is when you open the shutter. It's like opening your heart; the moment where you take something, and you give something. I can't explain it technically, but I think that if you don't live an emotion at this moment, if there is no energy passing from you and your subject, the picture will be boring." As you launch yourself into making your art, take a moment and go back to when you were eight, or whatever age shines brightest in your memory. What did your days look like then? Where was your east? What activity captivated your heart? Can you give yourself license to mirror some of that free expression as you fill the page or canvas?

Legend has it that "Hello It's Me" is the first song that Rock and Roll Hall of Fame nominee Todd Rundgren ever wrote. Let not this piece of history delude you. Your work in progress does not need to translate, daily, to some finished product or some fantastically swift achievement. There are 10,000 shades of the word "accomplishment." Be prepared that on most days work in progress will simply resemble some version of engaging with the principles presented in the last several chapters. Expect many days during which your mind will draw only blanks. That effort is still progress, and it is all part of the cumulative unclench! Just keep

> Expect many days where your mind draws only blanks. That effort is still progress, and it is all part of the cumulative unclench! JUST KEEP SHOWING UP. Rest assured, the muse will drop anchor.

showing up. Rest assured, the muse will drop anchor. When the Bulgarian-born artist Atanas Matsoureff communes with his watercolor paints, he aims to simply "leave traces," and he meets this intention by doing the work. "The best way to learn something is by doing," says he. "Once you discover things for yourself, they're yours, and nobody else can do them your way exactly."

Calling on objects and dreams and sorrows and scenes right in front of us can be a powerful springboard to populate a mind's vacant slate. In his *Letters to a Young Poet*, Rainer Maria Rilke tutors his apprentice friend, Franz Xaver Kappus, to "rescue himself" from the "general themes" in his poetry making. In order to do so, Rilke suggests instead that the young poet write with "heartfelt, silent, humble sincerity" about what everyday life is offering him. Imagine you are Franz and have just received this teaching.

Regularly, I lean on the teaching Rilke shared with Mr. Kappus. *What is everyday life offering you?* Record the weather, the soundtrack, the sadness, the joy, muted colors in a field, items on your desk, the bus stopped at the red light. **What just happened?** Your answer could take the simple shape of a list. Follow the threads of these observations and bring their plots into the art you begin to shape. Start with story, and be patient as one element leads to the next. Themes may sift in from the most pedestrian aspects of a day. The idea here is to seize what is right before you as a launch in; yield to that show and get swept up in its discovery.

Practice Seven — **Outtaking**

"Outtaking" is a ritual I employ in the pictures I make, and over time it's become sacrosanct in my life as an artist. It stems from my personal experience on assignment in the field where I would typically shoot a good forty or so frames in order to get that one "keeper," that one shot that sings, where the light is magical, and from which something of a story breaks through. The other thirty-nine images would have certain strengths, but they were not the "Aha" capture I was meant to make in that experience.

These cast-off pictures were my outtakes, always teaching me some small thing along the way

and nudging me into
a more fluid state.

This approach was not intentional
by any means. Believe me, it would
have been lovely to throw strikes at
frames one, two, or three. But I came
to understand that outtakes needed
to occur in order for me to unfold and
get completely present in my art.

Over time, I began to purposefully weave "outtaking" into my daily practice even when there were no assignments. Its merits are immeasurable, especially on those days when your imagination feels quiet.

In a free verse style, uninhibited by notions of results or finished products, "outtaking" looks a lot like rambling . . . creatively.

Think care free.

With your instrument(s) or materials in hand, go where the light takes you, letting color spill onto others, misspelling words, allowing the focus to be blurred, making mistakes, and ditching your "rule of thirds." You breathe and let the pour out be uncalculated, relieving yourself of the rigidity. Should you learn something from the work you produce in the midst of your outtaking, that's swell. But don't rely on it as the ticket in. Outtaking is meant as a warm-up activity whose purpose is to support you as you construct your daily routine. Allow yourself fifteen minutes or more to practice outtaking, then be done with these blurbs you express.

As a photographer, outtaking does not require much of an investment in terms of materials and such. If it happens to be that you are a sculptor, work with encaustics, or are engaged in a form of art that involves an abundance of elements, your outtakes might look like thumbnail sketches, tablet drawings, or a journaling of thoughts.

As this exercise serves as a prelude to your creating for real, adjust the variables in order to make it happen for you in a reasonable fashion. The assignment here is to make outtaking a nonnegotiable in your creative work for some succession of time. So experiment with how it sits for you.

EIGHT

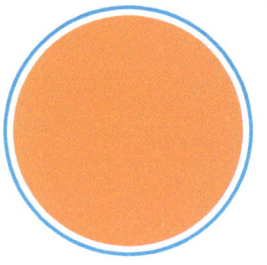

WHO CARES?

"Trying to please the audience lowers the level of sophistication constantly."
— Chögyam Trungpa

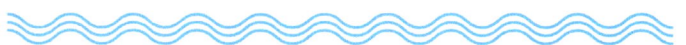

FOR THE FIRST TWENTY-FIVE YEARS OF HIS CAREER, Mark Rothko made his paintings on nights and weekends—due to his day job as a teacher—selling zero to few works well into the 1950s. During this chapter of his life, he simply had no interest in defending his work to an audience that could not understand him and his bolt from tradition. Rothko refused to let their confusion derail his world of imagination. So he continued his slow probe of layers and color blocks, insisting on a creative dialogue that included only him and his art. His canon of color fields and chapels and rooms is evidence of the beauty born in such small conversation. **"The most important tool the artist fashions through constant practice is the faith in his ability to produce miracles when they are needed,"** suggested the painter. Rothko, in his discipline and his refusal to let his brushstroke be directed by applause, remains a powerful illustration of what is possible when we keep faith in our own brand.

We make art to move ourselves and possibly to move others. In staying true to the former, we make the work that at some point may achieve the latter. Losing the "please" factor liberates our practice and process and opens a truth fluency in our creative pursuits. It is how we get to extraordinary. Yet today's culture wields a crushing pressure to put our name on the map, to achieve "influencer" status, to go viral... at once. Falling for colossal orders such as these as our navigation points detours us from creating the beauty we were born to make. Art was not meant to be a popularity contest.

So how ***does*** one dial down the volume on fashion and disengage from its often false hope? Watch what happens when you try an audience reframe, when you shed the weight of fashion and fame and embrace a "who cares" approach. Rothko cared, and that was all that mattered in those moments when his brush stroked the canvas. Begin with your audience of one. Discover that self. **"I write entirely to find out what I'm thinking, what I'm looking at, what I see and what it means,"** confessed Joan Didion in her *New York Times Book Review* essay entitled, "Why I Write." When you begin with that slow build, that uncomplicated ambition to move only yourself, your process is fueled organically.

There will come a time when you will know with a sureness of heart that the work is ready to be shared. As you sense this mark, consider the small circles of community where you feel as though you have been heard historically. This may be a circle of but two or three. Be grateful for any tribe that begins to gel. Just continue to make your music or dance or pottery or needlepoint without any expectations for a podium finish. Pay close attention to who your fans are. Trust that this cluster may introduce your work to friends who possess a shared sensibility. As that branching out happens, begin to nudge this community's footprint a bit. This can be done organically by building a simple website, curating a thoughtful social media presence, compiling an email list, exploring opportunities for sharing your work publicly at a local gallery, or creating an event. Engage fully among settings of kindred spirits, swapping contact information and other resources for exposure and community building. Offering your time and talent to others by teaching creative workshops is another viable course of action for expanding your tribe. What publications are you reading? Are there opportunities among those pages to share a guest contribution? Just as you dedicate practice time to create, commit to some small amount of time on a regular basis to focus on how you might share the art you are making.

 Marketing does not have to look loud. There will be little "selling" required of your art if in it you have made an investment that is authentic, and you have set aside the urgency factor. A circle of two or three will swell in time, and in that expansion you'll enjoy a grounding and sense of dignity that far outweighs the status of having 10K followers. Remember the breath taking from chapter seven? As you well know, that effect is not something one can orchestrate in advance by trying to please. Make work that is true, and trust it will snatch up the breath and bring a joy to those for whom it is meant.

Practice Eight — Artist Statement

The dreaded artist statement—its crafting continues to torture one and all. Here's a chance to practice yours. In doing so, you can begin to tease out a potential audience for your work. I always recommend, prior to beginning this exercise, a thoughtful review of statements made by other artists. By attending exhibits (online or in person), referencing art books, or Googling "artist statements," you will find many. Then, set aside some quiet time to empty the mind and breathe a bit. Have handy a notebook or keyboard. This is only practice; remind yourself of this repeatedly. It will free you up to tell the truth.

Before putting the pen to the page, sit with the artwork you have been making.

Breathe it in. For some moments, be its audience. Let the work speak to you. In what ways does it open you up? Take that information with you as you begin to prepare the statement of you and this work.

Brief is best. An artist statement is not a resume. Some relevant biographical information is wise, then move into your thought process. What rich details can you share? Who or what are your influences? Quotes can level up or even launch artist statements. Is there an environment essential to the work that you make? In the simplest of sentences, spell out why YOU are the person to make this particular art. Use your imagination to tell a story to your small circle. They are curious to know more.

NINE

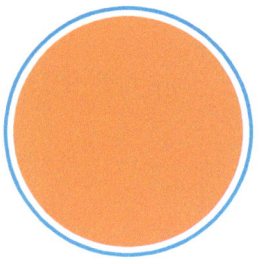

SHARE THE MERIT

"None of us can ever know the value of our lives, or how our separate and silent scribbling may add to the amenity of the world if only how radically it changes us, one and by one."
—Mary Karr

INTEGRAL TO THE SUPERFLOW SEQUENCE IS putting your work out there to be experienced by others. What if "useful" were the new "productive"? What if, instead of obsessing over going viral and amassing a laundry list of high regard, you dreamt smaller? I'm not implying that artists should not be compensated for their work. But I am suggesting that there's an ocean of possibility and freedom in the re-frame of art as a service to others. There's a big wide audience out there that many of us simply are ***not*** reaching.

A typical yoga class concludes with a period of rest known as *savasana*. In this finish to practice, students are welcome to melt into their mats, breathe easy, and reflect. The instructor invites the class to take whatever light or joy they may have generated through their effort and spread it out into the world, use it to be a lamp to a stranger, sister, or spouse. The customary cue is to "share the merit." This language immediately triggers a shift from "me" to "we" and can swiftly enhance one's humility and shared sense of purpose. It's a cheer for all.

With a nod to the old master painters, from the 1950s through the 1980s, photographer Saul Leiter—working under the radar—created a great and important archive of images depicting the opera of life on the streets of New York City. In terms of his regard as an artist, it's been said that he always **"found it comfortable to be ignored."** Might we do well to model such aspirations? Podium-type finishes have come to fuel the work of so many creatives, and often I question how this dilutes the integrity of the work itself? We invest so much time and effort into teasing out our authentic voice, only to allow its deflection to the background by our high hopes for that book deal, solo exhibit, or starring role. We could plot less and, in so doing, weaken the power that particular drive has over our work.

When one is "ignored," the spotlight is directed elsewhere and you (the artist) are free. Free to frame peculiar scenes, merge unfamiliar layers, and paint in clashing hues . . . minus the weight of the preferences of others. What if you were to exhale your joyful noise in a currency of gladness without the constraints of monetization and trade? When

> There's an ocean of possibility and freedom in the reframe of art as a SERVICE to others.

you strip the status stamp from the art, you make space in the spirit for possibility and imperfection and non-conformity. By all means, submit your work for consideration at the art gallery or the literary journal. Go for those heights, but also keep an awareness of the glimmer in less coveted, less considered markets.

Mary Ann Evans, in the pages of *Middlemarch*, asked, **"What do we live for, if it is not to make life less difficult to each other?"** "Sharing the merit" takes that swerve on completing the circle of the art you make. There is great joy to be experienced in beaming the beauty you see back out into the world, especially when it is done through the lens of service to others. Swiping another line from the pages of *Middlemarch:* it **"changes the lights for us."**

In your newly heightened creative life, you may find yourself sitting on some cheer that could be of much benefit to someone you never considered. "Sharing the merit" challenges us to get imaginative in terms of those unseen audiences whose spirits we might lift by freely offering our song, our stained glass, or our pottery. Any artist will testify to the fact that there is a feeling of being blessed as you stand before a work of art that you have made. Reflecting again on the insights of author and Rabbi Ariel Burger, **"A blessing is something that's heavy, and at the same time, it lifts us up."** Perhaps, through a creative life, such riddles are solved. Blessed ***and*** a blessing . . . imagination offers us the spout to be both.

Practice Nine — Be a Lamp

Make a date with some of the art you are beginning to create. Set aside the paint brush or camera or computer. Just take your composed mind and sit with the art as it is. Notice what you notice. As you do, begin to think of all the places it could go. In this exploration, go beyond the creative and personal circles in which you travel. Are there organizations in your community where you volunteer your time? Where did you attend college? Is there a hospital or library or community center local to you? Is there a social service agency from which you have benefited. Any and all of these might be communities where you can give back by sharing your art.

Go deeper with this probe. Imagine performing your music or teaching photography at a local after-school program. Does your local library house any study rooms or common areas whose walls your watercolors might grace? Does your United Way chapter need new headshots for their staff? How about your alumni magazine— how might your poetry read printed on page 36?

Make a list of five prospects for being a blessing, and then have at it.

TEN

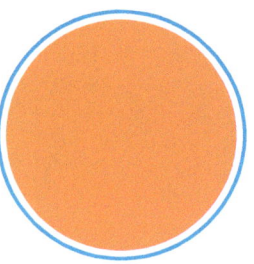

ENCORE!

> *"The channel is always there...and, it is our business to keep it open, to have access to the deepest part of ourselves."*
>
> —Saul Bellow

THE STAND-UP PADDLER STALKS STILL WATERS IN order to best compose and propel his or her personal flotation device (PFD) along the ocean's surface. But the surfer... with his board he forages fast wind and that large fetch. Conditions make all the difference in terms of their performance, and they tend not to settle for anything less than optimal. What would be the point? As hammered home in these past nine chapters, same goes for our artistic adventures.

Now is a wonderful time to thank yourself for chiseling out a creative clearing in your life and harvesting those conditions in which you will make your best art. The odds of your setting sail in an exalted manner have been greatly enhanced as a result of the time and effort you've invested. I promise! Soak up any sense of accomplishment you may be experiencing! It is also a perfect opportunity to take some stock in the cues by which you have been guided over these nine **SUPERFLOW** limbs. What impact has the experience had on your creative process? Take a moment to exhale and celebrate what came of your effort and commitment.

By now, you have gathered that this is not a book of "musts." The **SUPERFLOW** sequence, however, is powered by reiteration. There is no finish. On the heels of your "celebrating," it's time to return to chapter one! ***Patterns of purpose, upon repetition, deflect the dust.*** While you may be tempted to skim this final chapter... think twice. Its directions are every bit as essential as were those connected with the first nine pillars of the sequence. **SUPERFLOW** is not a one-shot approach. Each time you retrace its steps, you are a different person, and there are many wonderful discoveries to be met on each trip through its process. For example, it is likely that your "song of yourself" has in some way shifted during the course of your engaging with the practices in this book. Or maybe your schedule is such that your "time out" slice of the day looks like 9 p.m., where previously it fell at sunrise? Perhaps you've been introduced to a magnificent new route for sorting yourself out. There are seasons, and they turn.

Magic happens in the repeat. I encourage you to see for yourself... again and again. New epiphanies await you on future travels through the **SUPERFLOW** sequence, and its wide margins invite

> Patterns of purpose, upon repetition, deflect the dust.

you to customize each new interaction with its process. There are 10,000 ways to go free style as you return to page eighteen. It could be something as simple as recruiting a creative pal to join you in experiencing the book's ten practices. Regardless of the shape of each pass through, the repetition will begin to stamp out a nature in you that will shift you to flow in an autopilot mode in a less cluttered mind state. Each time you pick back up with projects (new and existing), likely you'll enjoy a heightened confidence and intuition in its next iteration.

SUPERFLOW was designed intentionally to get straight to the point. In your hands, its pages are meant to be well worn. I realize there may not be so much glamor in the verb "repeat," but that's what it takes to build habits—in this case skillful ones. There is no substitution for the work. In reapplying ourselves to the **SUPERFLOW** sequence, we keep open our channel that is *always* there. Go take new breaths, stay astonished, embrace those things you do not yet know, and continue to honor the work in progress that you are.

> Go take new breaths, STAY ASTONISHED, embrace those things you do not yet know, and continue to honor the work in progress that you are.

Practice Ten — **Report Card**

I'm not a fan of score keeping, particularly when it comes to the arts. There are, however, exceptions to be made.

This report card is for your eyes and ears only. It offers a chance to take stock, to reflect back on the creative state you found yourself in at the start of this process, and to note any news.

Arrange a small clearing in your day to pause and direct some attention to your experience engaging with the **SUPERFLOW** sequence. Perhaps you might do so in your studio or in some other space that allows you to be among your art's energy.

With intention, take your awareness inward, sighing out any distractions not of service to you. Open up to a blank page in your journal or some other white space where you might record some thoughts. Absent of any agenda, just begin to recall your adventure navigating each of the previous nine **SUPERFLOW** pillars:

- Song of Yourself
- Subtraction
- Groundwork … Branching In
- Composing … Poise of Mind
- Breath Taking
- THOREAUING
- Work in Progress
- Who Cares
- Share the Merit

You are the teacher here. How would you grade your personal experience in each of these nine chapters? In doing so, you might ask yourself questions such as:

Where did you stumble?
Where did you shine?

Were there practices that felt like home?

At which limbs did you feel your best self really show up?

Which chapters did you resist?

This exercise is not about beating up on yourself. **Be kind.**

There are valuable teachings in the epiphany moments and in the tangles that surface in self-study. Imagine how this intel can inform your pacing and your process on subsequent engagements with the **SUPERFLOW** sequence.

Then, once you have completed your self-grade,

open your calendar and

book a date
to launch your
SUPERFLOW encore!

CONCLUSION

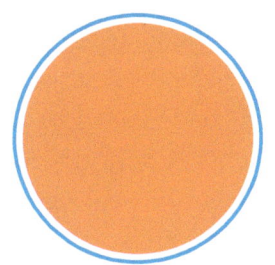

EMPTY PLATES AT THE DINNER TABLE GENERALLY indicate some level of success on the part of the recipe used to execute the dish. So what does the chef do if he or she is genuinely looking out for you? She shares the recipe. Everyone wins.

The **SUPERFLOW** sequence is a structure of principles intended as a game plan for reclaiming a bit of you, a doorway into living your purpose. I share this approach for lighting up the artist in you not because I claim to be an authority figure of any sort. But there is tremendous satisfaction in making one's formula for breakthrough available to another. In its application, I continue to personally witness small **SUPERFLOW** epiphanies both in my own creative endeavors and in the pursuits of countless other artists and artists-to-be. Empty plates!

So with you I share the recipe, and I invite you to make it all your very own. Go see what beautiful looks like for you. Go experience what flow feel likes. Again and again . . .

THANK YOU

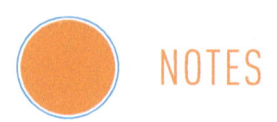

"I've always felt like there's also the silent majority of goodness; of generativity."
—Krista Tippett

ACKNOWLEDGMENTS

ART, LIKE LOVE, KEEPS MY WORLD GOING AROUND. I'm ever grateful for the teachers and notes of grace that remind me to keep at it. Much applause to these authors and their wisdom that remains a steady companion along my creative path:

Boorstein, Sylvia. *Happiness Is an Inside Job: Practicing for a Joyful Life.* Tabor, 1989.

Evans, Mary Ann. *Middlemarch.* Penguin, 2012.

Hirshfield, Jane. *Nine Gates: Entering the Mind of Poetry.* Harper Perennial, 1998.

Kornfield, Jack. *A Path with Heart.* Bantam, 1993.

Oliver, Mary. *A Poetry Handbook*. Mariner, 1994.

Popova, Maria. www.brainpickings.org.

Rilke, Rainer Maria. *Rilke's Book of Hours*. Riverhead, 2005.

Smith, Patti. *Devotion*. Yale University Press, 2017.

Thoreau, Henry David. *A Year in Thoreau's Journal*. Penguin, 1993.

Tippett, Krista. *Becoming Wise*. Penguin, 2017.

Trungpa, Chögyam. *True Perception: The Path of Dharma Art*. Rev. ed. Shambhala, 2008.

Thank you also to my family, to my editor and publisher, Christine Brooks Cote, and to the many artists and students with whom I teach and learn.

REPURPOSES

[19] Ben Platt quote... excerpted from the *92nd Street Y* podcast, episode: "Ben Platt in Conversation with Judith Light," October 2019.

[22] Jon Kabat-Zinn comment... as shared in the *Ten Percent Happier* podcast with host Dan Harris, episode: "National Trauma—Now What?" January 8, 2021.

[47] The musician Andrew Bird's story... originally told through the *Meditative Stories with Rohan Gunatillake* podcast, episode: "Listening to the Space Around You," May 20, 2020.

[53] David Whyte quote... excerpted from the *On Being* podcast, episode: "David Whyte: The Conversational Nature of Reality," April 2016.

[55, 91] Ariel Burger quotes... excerpted from the *On Being* podcast, episode: "Be a Blessing: Ariel Burger," February 2021.

[77] Atanas Matsoureff quote . . . excerpted from "Layers of Time," by Ani Kodjabasheva, *Artists Magazine*, January 2021.

[90] Saul Leiter comment . . . relayed to Max Kozloff in the introduction to *Saul Leiter (Photofile)*, Thames & Hudson, 2008.

[109] Krista Tippett quote . . . excerpted from the *On Being* podcast, episode: "Be a Blessing: Ariel Burger," February 2021.

ABOUT THE AUTHOR

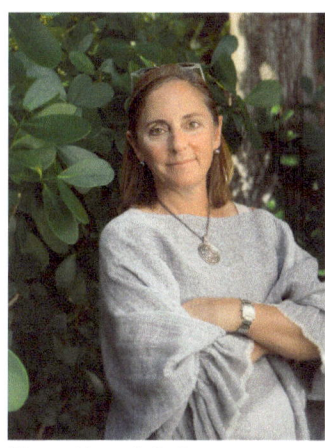
Photo: Hannah S. Currie

SUSAN CURRIE is a West Palm Beach-based poet with a camera. Her words and images have been widely exhibited and published. She met her muse some time ago when she discovered the ancient eight-limbed practice of yoga. Its way of life continues to inform and imprint the art she makes. The creative workshops she offers throughout the country share her signature approaches for practicing mindfulness in order to connect more authentically with one's creative voice. Susan is the author of three books —*Once Divided, Gracenotes,* and *Breathtaking* (Shanti Arts Publishing, 2016, 2017, 2019)—and the creator of CHARMCODES.

- www.susancurriecreative.com
- www.charmcodes.com

Shanti Arts

Nature ▪ Art ▪ Spirit

Please visit us online
to browse our entire book catalog,
including poetry collections and fiction,
books on travel, nature, healing, art,
photography, and more.

Also take a look at our highly
regarded art and literary journal,
Still Point Arts Quarterly, which
may be downloaded for free.

www.shantiarts.com

www.ingramcontent.com/pod-product-compliance
Lightning Source LLC
Chambersburg PA
CBHW040219220526
45473CB00001B/48